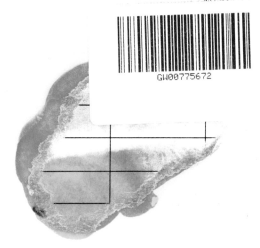

TRY IT AGAIN

A One Act Play

by

J. B. PRIESTLEY

SAMUEL FRENCH

LONDON

NEW YORK TORONTO SYDNEY HOLLYWOOD

GB 573 02279 8

MADE AND PRINTED IN GREAT BRITAIN BY
LATIMER TREND AND CO LTD, PLYMOUTH
MADE IN ENGLAND

CHARACTERS

COLIN ARLOTT
KRAMER
MRS ARLOTT
CLARE ARLOTT
HELEN CONNOR
MISS GILBERT

The action takes place in the drawing-room of Mrs Arlott's country house, late on a September evening, at the present time

TRY IT AGAIN

SCENE—*The drawing-room of a country house. Evening.*
It can be of any shape and style of decoration preferred by the producer so long as it has large french windows up C and a door either in the L or R wall. There is a sofa RC, an armchair down R and an armchair up LC. This furniture may be altered at the producer's discretion.

(*See the Ground Plan at the end of the play*)

When the CURTAIN *rises it is a warm September night and the french windows are open. Nothing can be seen outside them—a small black velvet backing is suggested—as the room is brilliantly lit.* MRS ARLOTT, *an elderly woman with a strong character, her son* COLIN, *an attractive but weakish man about thirty-five, his wife* CLARE, *a sensible and fairly attractive woman about thirty, and* HELEN CONNOR, *a very handsome and sophisticated woman in her early thirties, are all discovered in the room.* HELEN *is seated in the armchair* LC, MRS ARLOTT *at the* L *end of the sofa,* COLIN *at the* R *end of the sofa, and* CLARE *in the armchair down* R. *Nothing is said for a moment or two so that the audience may take in the scene. Nobody is relaxed, though* HELEN *is making a good shot at appearing so, and all look either angry or anxious. The most embarrassed and despairing character is, of course, the man,* COLIN. *The pause must be nicely timed and so played by the four that we do not feel anything has come to an end.*

CLARE (*to Mrs Arlott*) Well, it seems I must say it . . .
MRS ARLOTT. Say what, dear?
CLARE (*taking the plunge*) That you shouldn't interfere. It would be much better for all of us if you left us alone to settle our affairs in our own way.
HELEN. I couldn't agree more.

MRS ARLOTT (*stifling her anger*) And is that your opinion too, Colin?

COLIN (*embarrassed but at bay*) I'm afraid it is, y'know, Mother. After all . . .

MRS ARLOTT (*cutting in, scornfully*) No, not "After all" —which merely means you're going to give us one of your vague rambling speeches. And I don't think the rest of us have the time or patience to listen to it.

HELEN. Again, I couldn't agree more.

MRS ARLOTT (*losing her temper*) Oh—do stop making that stupid ill-bred remark.

HELEN. Certainly. But if we're going to talk about breeding and manners, I'd like to say something.

(MRS ARLOTT *tries to interrupt*)

(*Checking her with a more forceful tone*) No, and you're not going to stop me. I'm a guest here. I didn't force my way in, I was asked to come. It wasn't my idea. It wasn't Colin's . . .

COLIN. My hat—no!

HELEN (*to Mrs Arlott*) It was your idea. And from the moment I arrived, six hours ago, you've hardly been barely civil to me. If I'd come down by car instead of by train, I'd have pushed off before dinner. I don't enjoy staying with anybody who clearly regards me as a dose of poison. And if this is a sample of your good breeding and manners . . .

CLARE (*cutting in*) Oh—what does it matter? I agree that she hasn't been very nice to you, but what could you expect? All this is beside the point. Now that we've got so far, let's have it out properly—or give it up and stop talking.

COLIN. That's the only thing to do—pack it up.

CLARE. Yes, of course—you *would* think that!

HELEN. So would any man, if *I* know anything about them . . .

CLARE (*cattily*) And nobody denies you do.

HELEN. A good try, but you're not scoring anything. I think a woman's a fool if she doesn't understand men.

MRS ARLOTT. Possibly. Nevertheless, I don't think

you understand Colin, who happens to be my son. Which is one reason—and this *is* the point, Clare—that I've chosen to interfere, as you call it. You tell me I ought to have left you alone to settle your own affairs in your own way. But it's obvious you can't settle your own affairs. And this concerns me just as much as it does you, perhaps more. Colin is my only child. You can find yourself another husband, if necessary. I imagine that Miss Connor can easily find herself another lover. But I have no other son. And if Colin is unhappy, then I am unhappy. So I felt it was time I *did* interfere.

COLIN. Won't work, though. Sorry, Mother, but it won't, y'know.

MRS ARLOTT. Certainly it will. And the best thing you can do, Colin, is to leave us for an hour.

HELEN. If he goes, then I'm going.

CLARE (*hotly*) That's ridiculous . . .

MRS ARLOTT. And, of course, quite irresponsible. Probably typical.

HELEN (*stung*) Look—don't start saying what's typical about me. You don't know enough. In fact, you don't know anything . . .

MRS ARLOTT. I know that for the past year or so you've been Colin's mistress—and have done your best to break up what could have been a happy marriage . . .

HELEN. Don't talk that nonsense. It simply won't do. There may be women who break up happy marriages, but I've never met one. If Colin had been happily married he wouldn't have wanted me . . .

MRS ARLOTT. Perhaps he didn't . . .

HELEN. Of course he did. Before I wanted him. And when you talk about my being irresponsible, you either forget or don't know that I happen to earn my living— and it's quite a good living, too, and nothing that Colin could offer me would make me stop earning it . . .

CLARE. Then why couldn't you leave him alone?

HELEN. Because he fell in love with me. (*To Colin*) Didn't you?

(COLIN *hesitates miserably*)

CLARE. Well—go on—say it. Or can't you when your mother's here?

COLIN (*unhappily*) Yes, I did.

MRS ARLOTT (*reproachfully*) Oh—Colin! How could you?

HELEN. Why shouldn't he?

MRS ARLOTT (*with forced coolness*) Because, Miss Connor, although Clare has her faults and has never really understood my son, she is a far more suitable wife for him than you would ever be.

CLARE (*with a touch of bitter irony*) Thank you!

HELEN (*to Mrs Arlott; coolly*) You know, I doubt that. He's rather a weak character——

(COLIN *tries to protest*)

—(*turning to him*) yes, you are, darling—it's an essential part of your charm—(*to Mrs Arlott*) and he needs a wife who knows her way about. As I do. But what you don't seem to understand is that I've never offered myself to him as a wife. I'm not husband-hunting—I'm what is called a career woman—and if I was in search of a husband I'd want somebody with more weight than poor Colin has . . .

CLARE (*angrily*) What a horrible thing to say! If you really loved him you couldn't talk like that.

COLIN (*with angry irony*) Don't mind me, anybody! My God—you women!

HELEN. My dear, I know what you mean. I've often felt it myself. We're horrid brutes when we really get going, and the more female we are the worse we are. Still you can't shuffle out of *everything*, darling. Must face the facts sometime.

CLARE. For once I agree with you. And we'll settle this tonight.

COLIN (*angrily*) Settle *what*?

CLARE. Either you go away with her—or you finish with her for ever and stay with me.

HELEN. Unless, of course, he drops both of us and goes back to Mum.

CLARE. Yes, there's that, of course.

HELEN. It's on the cards, I think, dear. In fact, I can see it coming.

COLIN. Nonsense!

CLARE. I wonder.

MRS ARLOTT. All I'm concerned about is Colin's happiness. Naturally I wouldn't have arranged this—meeting—which is probably even more distasteful to me than it is to any of you—if I hadn't known for some time that he was intensely miserable.

CLARE (*with bitter emphasis*) Not as miserable as I've been. But, of course, that's different.

MRS ARLOTT. You've no need to take that tone with me, Clare. Naturally, it's different. Colin comes first with me. He always has done . . .

HELEN. That's what you think. But probably if you got down to it, you'd find that what comes first with you is yourself . . .

MRS ARLOTT (*angrily*) Don't be impertinent!

HELEN. Oh—fudge! You're one of these possessive mothers. It sticks out a mile. You talk about a happy marriage. I bet it hadn't a dog's chance with you around.

CLARE. No, it hadn't.

MRS ARLOTT (*outraged*) *What!* How dare you!

CLARE (*stormily*) How dare I? Well, I haven't dared —up to now. But it happens to be true. You think it's my fault that Colin's had this affair—you've as good as said so.

COLIN. Oh—I thought it was supposed to be my fault . . .

CLARE. Please—Colin! (*To Mrs Arlott*) But it wasn't my fault—there was nothing I could have done. Even before she came along, it wasn't right—because he hadn't escaped from you . . .

MRS ARLOTT. Escaped from me? Why should he escape from me? I'm his mother. All I wanted was to see him happily settled . . .

CLARE. Yes, but not *too* happily settled. You hadn't really let him go.

MRS ARLOTT. That is not true—and you ought to be

ashamed of yourself for saying such a thing. If you'd tried to understand him . . .

CLARE. I *do* understand him. I dare say he said I didn't . . .

HELEN (*sardonically*) I've known worse, but of course he had to mention it.

COLIN (*with angry irony*) Couldn't you entertain them with a few of our more intimate talks?

HELEN. Yes, if necessary, Colin dear.

MRS ARLOTT (*acidly*) I hope he's beginning to see how cheap and common you can make yourself. And now please be quiet. I say again, Clare, that if you'd tried to understand him, if you'd followed my advice instead of going against it, no other woman could have taken him away from you . . .

HELEN. He took himself away. I didn't take him.

CLARE (*to Mrs Arlott*) There weren't any real roots. Not because we were wrong for each other but because you never let him go. He's always been trying to escape, but he's not strong enough. He married me to escape, and then when you spoilt a real relationship, he got me mixed up with you, and so tried to escape by having this affair with Helen. I don't think he's really in love with her, because you haven't left him enough honest emotion to be in love with anybody . . .

HELEN. Oh—I wouldn't say that . . .

CLARE (*cutting in, sharply*) I doubt if you'd recognize honest emotion if you saw it. So keep out of this. I see now you're not really important . . .

HELEN. What? I'm dragged here to be accused of robbing the doting mother and adoring wife of their helpless hypnotized darling man—and now I'm told I'm not really important . . .

CLARE. Yes. Because if it hadn't been you, it would have been somebody else—anybody . . .

COLIN. Certainly not. What do you take me for?

CLARE. For the only son of a strong-minded, possessive, jealous widow, who's never allowed him to stand on his own feet . . .

COLIN. That's rubbish, Clare.

Mrs Arlott. Thank you, Colin. I'm glad to know what you think of me, Clare. No wonder you've failed as a wife . . .

Clare (*hotly*) Yes, I did fail—but simply because I didn't have it out with you right at the beginning. I ought to have told you then: "He's mine now, so don't try to take him back. Let him go." That's what I ought to have said.

Mrs Arlott (*angrily*) Well, I should have known how to deal with such stupidity and impudence.

Clare. Oh—don't be so ridiculously grand.

Helen. Look—I thought you were going to settle which one of us kept him. Not my idea—yours—but hadn't we better get on with it?

Clare (*almost ready for tears*) Apparently it's between you two now . . .

Mrs Arlott. Certainly not. Colin knows very well he's been making a fool of himself. But, of course, if it would help him to stay with me . . .

Helen. I agree with Clare—I might as well call you Clare, don't you think?—he's had too much of you already.

Colin (*rising and suddenly asserting himself*) If you want to know, I've had too much of all three of you tonight. What the devil do you think I am? A parcel? I've never felt so damned humiliated in my life. You ought to have heard yourselves. Who keeps him? Who takes him? Whose is he? I've been described as weak, but I am not weak enough to take any more of this. Go on—settle it between you! Have a raffle, if you like. But don't think I'm going to stay here waiting for the verdict, when you've finished slanging each other. I'm clearing out—and don't ask me where because I don't know—and if I did, I wouldn't tell you.

Clare (*alarmed*) No—Colin—please!

Colin. I tell you, I've had enough. I'm going.

(*He is about to move when he is stopped by the voice of* Kramer *heard just outside the windows*)

Kramer (*off; peremptorily*) No—wait!

COLIN (*looking towards the windows; astonished*) What?

(KRAMER *enters through the french windows. He is an oldish, foreign-looking man, clean-shaven with a mane of grey hair. He is an authoritative formidable man, with a very impressive manner not without humour. He can have a slight foreign accent*)

KRAMER (*chiefly addressing Mrs Arlott*) Forgive me, please—but I felt that I must intrude. I am—*Kramer*.

HELEN (*impressed*) Oh yes—of course.

MRS ARLOTT (*rather annoyed*) I don't know why "of course".

KRAMER (*to Helen; twinkling*) You tell her—please.

HELEN. Mr Kramer is a world-famous producer of plays and director of films.

COLIN (*interested*) Oh—yes—*the* Kramer . . .

MRS ARLOTT (*dryly*) Well, we're much honoured, no doubt. I'm Mrs Arlott—the owner of this house. Do you usually enter strange houses uninvited, through the window, Mr Kramer?

KRAMER (*shrugging*) Of course not. The circumstances are—unusual. I have already asked you, remember, to forgive me.

MRS ARLOTT. Very well. You have lost your way perhaps?

KRAMER. No, no. I do not know the way—but I have a chauffeur out there who knows it.

MRS ARLOTT. Then I must ask you to leave us, Mr Kramer. This isn't an ordinary social occasion—we happen to be discussing intimate family affairs . . .

KRAMER (*beaming*) Yes, I know. I have been listening . . .

MRS ARLOTT (*annoyed*) Well—really . . .

HELEN (*suddenly amused*) How much have you heard, Mr Kramer?

COLIN. Not much, I hope.

KRAMER. I will tell you how much I have heard in a minute, when we begin to try the scene again . . .

MRS ARLOTT (*astounded*) "Try the scene again"? Do you know what you're talking about?

HELEN (*interested*) I'm sure he does, you know.

CLARE. Tell us what you mean, Mr Kramer.

MRS ARLOTT. But this is preposterous. A complete stranger—walking in . . .

KRAMER (*impressively, cutting in*) Mrs Arlott—the fact that I'm a complete stranger is in my favour. It is the complete stranger you need. Especially when he is—Kramer. But first, let me explain. The car stops—just out there. I hear voices—urgent voices—angry voices. Something is happening—not the usual small-talk. A scene. An unusual opportunity, especially among the English, who do not like scenes. And I am—Kramer. For forty years, in many different places, I have been directing scenes. So I listen. And my clever secretary, for whom I hold the torch, takes down in shorthand all that is said—for reference, you understand. (*He turns and calls*) Miss Gilbert!

(MISS GILBERT *enters through the french windows, cool and smiling, carrying a rather large notebook. She is a cheerful woman of about forty with spectacles*)

(*Introducing her*) Miss Gilbert. Mrs Arlott. Young Mrs Arlott—Clare, I think. Miss—er—Helen Connor. Right? Mr Colin Arlott. There—we are all introduced—it is all respectable.

MRS ARLOTT. No doubt. But it still seems to me preposterous—and a joke in very doubtful taste . . .

KRAMER (*weightily*) A joke? There is no joke, I assure you. This is serious to you and it shall be serious to me . . .

MRS ARLOTT (*angrily*) Mr Kramer, this is my house—and I must ask you to leave it, though not before your secretary has destroyed her shorthand notes . . .

KRAMER. Madam, I promise you that these notes will be destroyed when we leave here . . .

MISS GILBERT (*cheerfully*) I don't want them. I just took it all down on Mr Kramer's orders. But don't you send him away, Mrs Arlott. He won't do you any harm, I can promise you. He's a very remarkable man. (*She moves L of the french windows*)

HELEN. Of course he is. And even if he wasn't, he could hardly spoil this party.

KRAMER. Quite so. And I must remind you, Mrs Arlott, that already you owe me something . . .

MRS ARLOTT. Certainly not.

KRAMER. Yes, indeed. Aren't you forgetting that if I hadn't stopped him, your son would have left this house?

COLIN. That's true. Though I don't say I'm staying.

MRS ARLOTT. Very well, I'll admit that. But you must realize . . .

KRAMER (cutting in, smiling) Yes, yes—of course—all very private, very intimate, very embarrassing—though I think we need never be embarrassed if we really don't wish to be. *I* am never embarrassed.

MRS ARLOTT. That I can believe. But the presence of two strangers . . .

KRAMER. My dear Mrs Arlott—forget we are strangers. And remember that you were all exceedingly angry with one another—that you had reached a deadlock—that your son might have rushed out of this house in anger and despair, in a mood for any folly . . .

CLARE (in a low, grave tone) That's true.

COLIN. *I'm* not denying it.

KRAMER. Whatever I do can hardly make things worse.

HELEN. I couldn't agree more.

KRAMER. And it might make them much better. A man rushing out into the night, blind with fury. Three women left behind to accuse one another—to scream, to scratch, to bite. Surely we can do better.

CLARE. I agree, though I don't understand what you want to do.

COLIN. Neither do I, but I'll risk it.

MRS ARLOTT. Very well. Though I don't see that anything useful can be done.

KRAMER (moving down L) Well, let us try. Here, we will say, is a scene from a play—the *Private Lives of the Arlotts and Helen Connor*. I am directing it. We have the words. We have the actors . . .

MRS ARLOTT. But we are not actors.

KRAMER. Imagine you are. And indeed in one sense we are all actors. I tell you, I was thinking as I listened to you how you were all acting—playing the parts expected of you or that you had given yourselves. Not good acting, most of it. Bad theatre. Routine performances of routine parts. The doting mother. The injured wife. The clever, hard mistress. The bewildered badgered son, husband, lover. A mediocre comedy—but—and this I must impress upon you—perhaps with Tragedy waiting in the wings. As, at the last moment, you realized. (*He looks round at them, sternly*) Do not deny that you realized this. Let us have no pretending that Tragedy might not soon have claimed the stage.

CLARE. I know *I* felt that, Mr Kramer. We were angry—not getting anywhere—and Colin at the end was desperate. Then suddenly I was frightened. Yes, I'm grateful to you for stopping him. And I'll do whatever you want me to do. I'm sure we all will.

KRAMER. Thank you. But remember, please, for this little time, I am your director. You allow me to say what I want to say. You do not tell me I am insulting. It is all —you must understand—quite impersonal. We are trying to produce a good scene instead of a bad one. So—no standing on dignity—no "How dare you!" You are the players. I am the director. Now we try to improve the little piece. Where shall we start? Miss Gilbert?

MISS GILBERT (*tonelessly*) Mrs Arlott speaking. "I don't think you understand Colin, who happens to be my son. Which is one reason that I've chosen to interfere, as you call it . . ."

KRAMER (*to Mrs Arlott*) Do you remember the rest of that speech?

MRS ARLOTT. I remember the general sense of it. I told Clare . . .

KRAMER (*cutting in*) No, please. Now you tell her. Sometimes we must discuss the situation—but we begin with some acting. It is an important speech, Mrs Arlott. Perhaps you would like to stand—perhaps there . . .

(He indicates a good spot up stage C. Mrs Arlott, with the air of one who has condescended to play a childish game, rises and goes to it. But once she starts speaking, she loses this manner and is much as she was originally)

Mrs Arlott. I don't think you understand Colin, who happens to be my son. Which is one reason that I've chosen to interfere, as you call it. You say I ought to have left you alone to settle your own affairs. But you can't settle your own affairs. And this concerns me just as much as it concerns you, perhaps more. Colin is my only child. You can find yourself another husband, if necessary. Miss Connor can easily find herself another lover . . .

Helen *(rising; cutting in)* Hoy—I don't think you were quite as insulting as that, last time.

Miss Gilbert *(reading from her notes)* "I imagine that Miss Connor can easily find herself another lover."

Helen. That's better. It's emphasizing the "easily" that puts me in the tart class, where I honestly don't belong.

Mrs Arlott. . . . easily find herself another lover. But I have no other son. If Colin is unhappy, then I am unhappy. So I felt it was time I *did* interfere. *(She looks at Kramer)* Then Colin said something foolish about its not working, and I told him he'd better leave us. Not leave the house, of course, but to go into some other room. I thought we three women would get on better without him. And, of course, he was finding it all dreadfully embarrassing.

Kramer. Of course. Nevertheless, I think it was not good to suggest he should run and play—like a child.

Colin. That's what I felt.

Helen. That's where I said: "If he goes, then I'm going." It wasn't that I was afraid of being left with these two—I can take care of myself—but I felt if Colin wasn't in this room there was no reason why I should be here.

Mrs Arlott. I called that attitude irresponsible. I still do.

HELEN (*to Kramer*) That stung me, I'll admit. The next bit of the scene is me explaining myself. You needn't remind me, Miss Gilbert—I know what I said. But if we're cleaning this up—which I'm beginning to suspect is your idea—I'd like to explain myself without losing my temper or trying to get anybody's goat. All right?

KRAMER. Certainly. I said that sometimes we discuss the situation.

HELEN. I'm the editor of a fashion magazine—*The Smart Woman*. It's a good job and I adore it. Now what women like these two never understand is that women like me, who really work and like it, have a point of view of our own, quite different from theirs. They have the old female idea that every woman is trying to find a man to support her. But it's not my idea. I want a lover —yes. I suppose every normal woman does. But not a husband, nor a man to be with all the time. That's what they don't understand.

CLARE (*rising and moving above the armchair down* R) I do. I'm not so dense. In fact, I think it's you who are rather stupid about this. Don't you see that if you've taken my husband's interest, his emotions, his desire to be a lover, then you've taken *him*? The fact that he's only a sparetime hobby for you makes it all the harder to take. Can't you see that?

HELEN. Yes, dear, I can.

CLARE. And then when you ended by saying that if you wanted a husband, Colin wouldn't do—too light-weight or something—you made it even worse.

COLIN. You did for me. That was a very nasty one.

CLARE. Well, it was for me, too.

KRAMER. These are very good points, my friends. They come nearer the truth. They make us understand the scene better. Let us remember the final situation before. You three women were angry, unable to agree, ready to accuse one another of everything. No solution there. The man—Colin—is about to rush away, perhaps to drink too much, perhaps to find some other and much worse woman. And why? Because he not only feels embarrassed, ashamed, but also deeply humiliated, as if his essential manhood, his respect for himself, were being taken away . . .

COLIN (*to the three women*) He's absolutely right there, you know. That's exactly what I did feel. And I couldn't take it. No man could. Mother'd begun it by suggesting I was still her little boy. Helen made it worse by talking as if I were a sort of plaything, not good enough to take seriously . . .

HELEN. No, darling—be fair. I never said that. The point I was making was that I wasn't in the husband-market, as they seemed to think, and that if I ever did tie myself to a man, he'd have to be somebody very special, well in the heavy-weight class.

KRAMER. Reasonable—but not tactful, we will say. But you said something else to him, Miss Connor, that also would humiliate him. What was it, Miss Gilbert?

MISS GILBERT (*after a brief examination of her notes*) It's this, I fancy. "Still, you can't shuffle out of *everything*, darling. Must face the facts sometime."

HELEN. Yes, I remember. And wouldn't help his ego, I admit. But the truth is—I was irritated—and perhaps a bit humiliated myself, too—by the miserable way he was taking this female bullying. The kind of man I admire would have told us all to shut up and frightened us into doing it. (*To Kramer*) That's what *you'd* have done.

KRAMER. With you three—yes, easily. But with my own mother, wife, mistress—I doubt it.

COLIN. Thanks for that. They were certainly making me feel a worm, but a worm that was getting ready to turn. I think you took a hand then, Clare.

KRAMER. I think so, too. Something about settling it tonight—disposing of you between them.

CLARE. Yes, I was sorry afterwards I put it like that. It must have made him feel small, though at that moment I didn't mind if he did feel small. He'd hurt me—and I wanted to hurt him—yes, and in front of her. I must say we women really are *beastly* sometimes.

KRAMER. We all are in our different ways. And if we freely admit it then we begin to clear the air.

CLARE. I said: "Either you go away with her—or you

finish with her for ever and stay with me." And Helen
said: "Unless, of course, he drops both of us and goes
back to Mum."

HELEN. Right. Another foul little blow, I admit—that
going back to Mum.

COLIN. Yes, I could have smacked you across the jaw
for that one.

HELEN. Why didn't you? My kind of man would—
except that I'd never have dared say such a thing in
front of him.

CLARE. You know, Helen, you're now practically
telling us that Colin simply isn't your kind of man.

HELEN. Yes, dear, I am. That's how it's beginning to
look in what you might call this new Kramer atmos-
phere . . .

MRS ARLOTT (*coldly*) Which seems to be introducing
a strain of vulgarity into this discussion . . .

KRAMER (*persuasive but authoritative*) Mrs Arlott, please
do not talk of vulgarity. It is wrong. We are past the
point where things are vulgar or not vulgar. The lid is
off. The pots are coming to the boil. The truth is beginning to emerge. Now I have always believed, in work or
in life, that nothing good can be founded on lies, that
real creation and happiness depend on truth . . .

CLARE (*eagerly*) Oh—yes. I agree. I think I've always
felt that.

HELEN. I know it.

MRS ARLOTT (*sceptically*) Indeed!

HELEN (*angrily*) Yes, indeed.

KRAMER. No, no, no—Mrs Arlott, Miss Connor—I
don't want this kind of little scene. Nothing comes out
of it except that you are deeply antagonistic to each
other. And we know that already. You are opposing
types—different ages, social groups, habits, customs, view
points. That is clear and does not need to be stressed by
snarls and scratches. Let us keep to the main scene—the
deadlock reached by the women, the deep humiliation
of the man leading to flight . . .

CLARE (*urgently*) But *must* it end like that?

KRAMER. Ah—no—not at all. Already it is assuming

a different shape, a different tone. But this next part depends on you, I think?

CLARE (*startled*) On me?

KRAMER. Let me try to remember.

(MISS GILBERT *prepares to prompt him*)

No, Miss Gilbert—not yet. One moment. Yes, I remember. Miss Connor accused Mrs Arlott of being a possessive mother . . .

HELEN. And I said the marriage hadn't a dog's chance with her around . . .

KRAMER (*to Clare*) Then you, my dear, agreed. And when Mrs Arlott said, "How dare you!"—which we should never say to anybody, because it doesn't mean anything—you stormed at her. You remember?

CLARE. Yes, I really was angry then. But I spoke the truth. I meant what I said about Colin not having escaped. I'm sorry, Mr Kramer—I'd like to help—but I can't go back on that.

KRAMER. I haven't asked you to say anything else. But often much depends on *how* something is said. We resent the tone of voice more than we resent what the voice tells us. So this time make more or less the same speech but instead of an angry, bitterly resentful, accusing tone—try something easier, friendlier, regretful not accusing. And instead of glowering at her across the room, try going nearer and not raising your voice. Miss Gilbert—the cue, please.

MISS GILBERT (*reading her notes*) "You think it's my fault that Colin's had this affair—you've as good as said so . . ."

CLARE. Yes, I remember. (*She begins to move up stage closer to Mrs Arlott, using quite a different tone from her original speech—regretful, not unfriendly, rather persuasive*) You think it's my fault that Colin's had this affair— you've as good as said so . . .

COLIN (*to Kramer*) I came in here. (*To Clare*) Oh—I thought it was supposed to be my fault.

CLARE (*half-smiling*) Please—Colin! (*To Mrs Arlott, in in the same manner*) But it wasn't my fault. There was nothing I could have done. Even before she came along, it wasn't right—because he hadn't escaped from you . . .

MRS ARLOTT (*milder than originally*) Escaped from me? Why should he escape from me? I'm his mother. All I wanted was to see him happily settled . . .

CLARE (*in the same manner, with no bitterness*) Yes, but not too happily settled. You hadn't really let him go.

MRS ARLOTT. Here I think I told her that wasn't true —and that she ought to be ashamed of herself for saying such a thing. I can say it again, if you like, Mr Kramer, but somehow it doesn't sound right now.

KRAMER (*with a kind of innocent cheerfulness*) No, it doesn't, does it? Too quarrelsome—eh?

HELEN (*admiringly*) You're an artful old devil, you are! We just can't keep it up now.

KRAMER. Do you want to keep it up?

HELEN. Not me—no.

MRS ARLOTT. Then I told Clare that if she'd tried to understand Colin, no other woman could have taken him away from her.

CLARE. Then came my big speech—I was still terribly angry. (*To Miss Gilbert*) How did it start?

MISS GILBERT (*reading her notes*) There weren't any real roots. Not because we were wrong for each other but because you never let him go.

CLARE. Yes, I said he'd always been trying to escape but he wasn't strong enough. He married me to escape, found he couldn't, got me mixed up with his mother, so had to try to escape again—this time with Helen . . .

KRAMER. You still believe that?

CLARE. Yes, I do—up to a point. It doesn't allow anything to Helen for being so attractive. In fact, I said anybody would have done. That's silly, of course. And, of course, I realize Helen *is* very attractive . . .

HELEN. Well now, we're really making progress . . .

CLARE. And, of course, men aren't like us—they're easily attracted—wanting to make love to somebody different . . .

HELEN True enough. Except we aren't quite so unlike them as we love to pretend, dear. But I'm glad it's admitted now that I was quite a temptation. (*Smiling at him*) Um—Mr Kramer?

KRAMER. Oh—yes. Hard to resist, as I can see. But even so—if this affair was serious to our friend Colin . . .

COLIN. It was.

KRAMER. It must have been to have brought about such a conference. And I say, if it was serious, then there is much in what Clare has said—a psychological rather than a physical need. Always, I think we underrate the psychological and overrate the physical side of these affairs. But you have not finished, Clare, the little scene with Mrs Arlott.

CLARE. No, after some nasty bitter exchanges with Helen and Colin, which I'd just as soon forget, Mrs Arlott said no wonder I'd failed as a wife. Say it to me again, please, then I'll remember.

MRS ARLOTT (*easier now*) No wonder you've failed as a wife.

CLARE (*slowly and regretfully, not angrily*) Yes, I did fail. But simply because I didn't have it out with you right at the beginning. I ought to have told you then: "He's mine now, so don't try to take him back. Let him go." That's what I ought to have said.

MRS ARLOTT. Then I said something about stupidity and impudence. I'm afraid I lost my temper, dear.

CLARE. Yes, we both did. (*Turning to Kramer*) By the way, I see now I oughtn't to have talked that way in front of Colin. I mean—about his being mine—and her not taking him back—and all that. It does make him sound as if he were a sort of possession—not a real person . . .

COLIN. Yes, that's the point. All three of you talked like that—especially you and Mother. And anyhow Helen has made it pretty plain that she didn't take me very seriously. Bit much all of a sudden, y'know, Mr Kramer.

KRAMER. Hence your final impassioned speech.

COLIN. Quite. And I would have cleared out if you hadn't stopped me.

KRAMER. But that speech of yours was mostly wounded vanity . . .

COLIN (*rather offended*) Here—wait a minute. You said earlier—and quite truthfully too—that I felt my—er—essential manhood, my respect for myself, had been taken away.

KRAMER (*coolly*) Yes, that was there, too. I emphasized it specially for the ladies. But now that I am talking frankly to you, my friend, I tell you that your running-away speech was mostly dictated by wounded vanity, which always makes us want to run away. Remember you have had an adoring mother, a loving wife, a charming, intelligent mistress—which is far more than one man's share. And I think you would have run away to find somebody else to make a fuss of you. Of course we men all want plenty of fuss over us if we can find it . . .

MISS GILBERT (*surprising us all*) I know one man who does.

KRAMER (*grinning*) Attend to your notes, dear Miss Gilbert. But we must not ask for too much. We must take the rough with the smooth. Above all, we must not run away. That is not how we can assert our manhood, our self-respect . . .

COLIN (*protesting*) Yes, but three of them—all angry . . .

KRAMER. I know, I know—it would not be easy. But it is better to assert yourself, make your choice and not have it made for you, then have one woman on your side, respecting you—than still have three angry women against you.

COLIN. Yes, but I didn't know what to *do*. And it's all right your barging in and tidying up the scene you overheard, making it a bit more civilized . . .

CLARE. And truthful . . .

COLIN. Yes, truthful—but it's only one scene—and what's the plot? How does the play end?

HELEN. That's the stuff, Colin! It's what I've been wondering. Basically we're still where we were when you came in, Mr Kramer, even though our tempers may have cooled.

MRS ARLOTT. Quite true. Well, Mr Kramer?

KRAMER (*smiling*) But there is a limit to my inter-ference, my friends. It is your play—not mine. I would not presume . . . (*He hesitates*)

MISS GILBERT (*surprising us again*) Of course you would. Tell them. And don't ask me again to attend to my notes—because—look . . . (*She tears out the notes ostentatiously and throws them down*)

MRS ARLOTT (*relieved*) Thank goodness for that! Well, Mr Kramer—are you going to disappoint us now?

KRAMER. Possibly. I cannot guarantee satisfaction. But if it were my play—then I think this would be my solution, if I wanted something like a happy ending. (*He pauses a moment, dramatically, looking round at them*) The man would return to the wife. Not for conventionality, because they are already married, but because of the three women she loves him the most, for his own sake, and he will be happiest with her. And for her sake, as well as his own, this man will behave as a man and not as a spoilt child, devoting himself to her, discovering in her much that he has not yet found.

CLARE (*eagerly, looking at him*) Colin!

(COLIN *nods, then looks at Kramer*)

KRAMER (*impressively*) Each woman must give up something. The mother must let her son go, not wanting him at heart still to be her helpless child—but a man. That is essential. No happiness for either without it. (*He pauses*) The mistress must not press any demands upon a man who, whatever their relations may have been, is not the man she really wants, as she herself has said.

HELEN (*nodding*) Fair enough.

CLARE (*uncertainly*) And what about the wife? I can't see that she gives up anything.

KRAMER. Oh—yes. She does not say any more, "Either you go away with her—or you finish with her for ever." She does not play that little scene again, with all its jealousy and anger and ultimatums. If she knows he is hers and he happens to stray a little, as men will do, then she closes one eye—like a little wink that nobody sees except perhaps her guardian angel. For no doubt even guardian angels . . .

MISS GILBERT (*loud and clear*) Mr Kramer—we're going to be terribly late again.

KRAMER. Then we must go.

(MISS GILBERT *exits through the french windows during the next speech*)

Now try to sketch out the last act—and take it easy . . .

HELEN (*cutting in*) Mr Kramer—sorry to interrupt—but are you driving to London?

KRAMER. We are. You want a lift?

HELEN (*moving to the door* L) Yes, please.

(HELEN *exits* L)

KRAMER. Yes, take it easy—don't rush it. Try for truth—sincerity—real feelings. No routine performances of routine parts. No bad theatre. No mediocre comedy with tragedy waiting round the corner . . .

(HELEN *enters* L *with a coat and carrying a small bag*)

(*Giving Helen a grin*) Yes—you are a character they can do without now. But you think you can make a plaything of old Kramer—um?

HELEN (*cheerfully*) No—but I'd like to have a durned good try. (*Moving up to the french windows*) Good night, dears. Happy curtain!

(HELEN *exits through the french windows*)

KRAMER (*following Helen*) Good night. Good night. Best wishes. Good night . . .

KRAMER *exits. The others go to the windows calling* "*Good night*" *as—*

the CURTAIN *falls*

FURNITURE AND PROPERTY PLOT

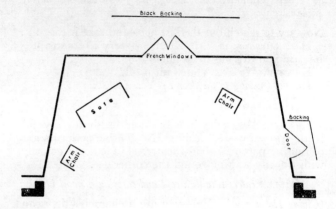

On stage: Sofa
           2 armchairs

Off stage: Coat, small bag (HELEN)

Personal: MISS GILBERT: notebook, spectacles

NOTE ON COSTUME

If necessary everybody can be in day clothes, but it might be better if Mrs Arlott and Clare are wearing simple evening frocks, Colin a dinner jacket, and Helen is wearing smart town day clothes. Kramer and Miss Gilbert are wearing travelling clothes to suit their respective types.

LIGHTING PLOT

PROPERTY FITTINGS REQUIRED: Centre light, with table lamps and standard lamps at the producer's discretion (all practical)

A drawing-room
Interior. Evening

THE MAIN ACTING AREAS are by the french windows (up C), by the sofa (RC), by the armchair (R), and by the armchair (L)

THE APPARENT SOURCE OF LIGHT is from those practical lamps used

OFF STAGE LIGHTING: darkness outside french windows; strip outside door

To open: bright artificial lighting
No cues